50 GREAT STATES

LEVEL **3** READER

READING LEVEL
3
GRADES 2 TO 4

The 50 STATES

Our flag has fifty stars—
one for each of the fifty
states!

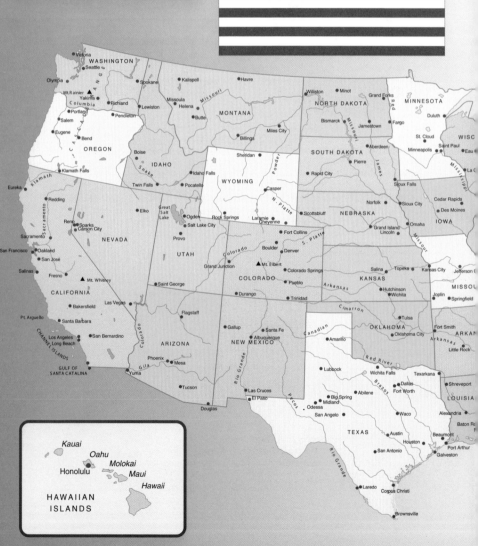

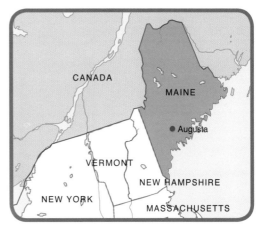

What a big, beautiful country we have! It's made up of fifty great states, each unique and each fun to visit! Let's start with the most eastern state in the country—Maine.

Maine (ME)

Capital: Augusta

Nickname: Pine Tree State

Bird: Chickadee

Flower: White pine cone and tassel

Eastport, Maine, is the most eastern city in the U.S. It is the first city in the country to see the rays of the morning sun.

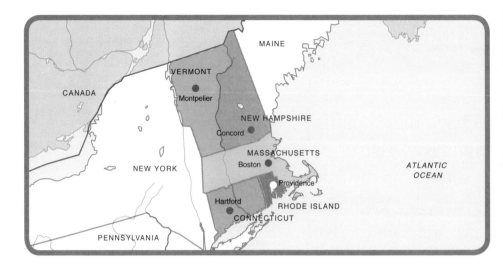

Vermont (VT)

Capital: Montpelier
Nickname: Green Mountain State
Bird: Hermit thrush
Flower: Red clover

Vermont makes more maple syrup than any other state.

New Hampshire (NH)

Capital: Concord
Nickname: Granite State
Bird: Purple finch
Flower: Purple lilac

Alan B. Shepard, Jr., was the first American to go up into space. He was born in New Hampshire.

Massachusetts (MA)

Capital: Boston

Nickname: Bay State

Bird: Chickadee

Flower: Mayflower

The first basketball game was played in Springfield, Massachusetts, in 1891.

Rhode Island (RI)

Capital: Providence

Nickname: Ocean State

Bird: Rhode Island red hen

Flower: Violet

Rhode Island is the smallest state. It covers an area of 1,214 square miles.

Connecticut (CT)

Capital: Hartford

Nickname: Constitution State

Bird: Robin

Flower: Mountain laurel

Connecticut is a Native-American word meaning "Place beside a long river."

New York (NY)

Capital: Albany

Nickname: Empire State

Bird: Eastern Bluebird

Flower: Rose

Part of the great Niagara Falls is in New York. The rest is in Canada.

Pennsylvania (PA)

Capital: Harrisburg

Nickname: Keystone State

Bird: Ruffed grouse

Flower: Mountain laurel

Hershey's® chocolates are made in the yummy-smelling town of Hershey, Pennsylvania.

New Jersey (NJ)

Capital: Trenton

Nickname: Garden State

Bird: Eastern goldfinch

Flower: Purple violet

Thomas Edison invented or perfected the lightbulb, telephone, and phonograph in Menlo Park, New Jersey.

Delaware (DE)

Capital: Dover

Nicknames: First State; Diamond State

Bird: Blue hen chicken

Flower: Peach blossom

Delaware is called the First State. It was the first to agree to the U.S. Constitution and join the new country.

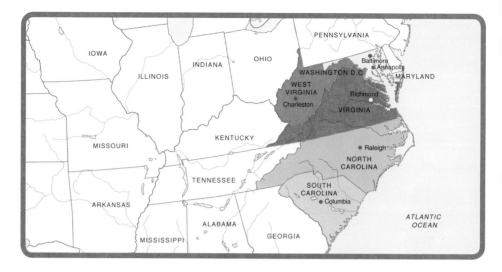

Maryland (MD)

Capital: Annapolis

Nickname: Old Line State

Bird: Baltimore oriole

Flower: Black-eyed Susan

Francis Scott Key wrote "The Star-Spangled Banner" while bombs were bursting in air over Fort McHenry, Maryland, during the War of 1812.

West Virginia (WV)

Capital: Charleston

Nickname: Mountain State

Bird: Cardinal

Flower: Rhododendron

Golden Delicious apples were first grown in Clay County, West Virginia.

Virginia (VA)

Capital: Richmond
Nickname: The Old Dominion
Bird: Cardinal
Flower: American dogwood

Jamestown, Virginia, was the first English town in the future U.S. It was founded in 1607.

North Carolina (NC)

Capital: Raleigh
Nickname: Tar Heel State
Bird: Cardinal
Flower: Flowering dogwood

In 1903, the Wright Brothers made the first successful manned airplane flight at Kitty Hawk, North Carolina.

South Carolina (SC)

Capital: Columbia
Nickname: Palmetto State
Bird: Great Carolina wren
Flower: Yellow jessamine

Coward, Ninety Six, and Welcome are all towns in South Carolina.

Georgia (GA)

Capital: Atlanta

Nickname: Peach State

Bird: Brown thrasher

Flower: Cherokee rose

The Great Okefenokee Swamp in Georgia is the biggest swamp in North America.

Florida (FL)

Capital: Tallahassee

Nickname: Sunshine State

Bird: Mockingbird

Flower: Orange blossom

Everglades National Park, in southern Florida, is home to alligators, manatees, and rare birds.

Alabama (AL)

Capital: Montgomery

Nicknames: Yellowhammer State;
The Heart of Dixie

Bird: Yellowhammer

Flower: Camellia

Many kids go to Space Camp at the U.S. Space and Rocket Center in Huntsville, Alabama.

Mississippi (MS)

Capital: Jackson

Nickname: Magnolia State

Bird: Mockingbird

Flower: Magnolia flower

The Choctaw Indians of Mississippi played stickball—the oldest game in the U.S.

Louisiana (LA)

Capital: Baton Rouge

Nickname: Pelican State

Bird: Eastern brown pelican

Flower: Magnolia

Rayne, Louisiana, is known as "The Frog Capital of the World."

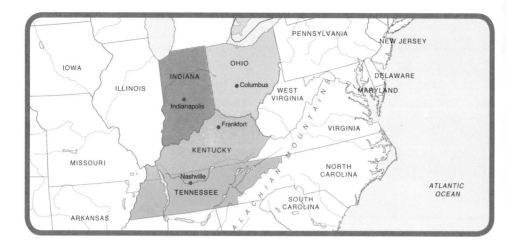

Ohio (OH)

Capital: Columbus

Nickname: Buckeye State

Bird: Cardinal

Flower: Scarlet carnation

The Pro Football Hall of Fame is in Canton, Ohio.

Indiana (IN)

Capital: Indianapolis

Nickname: Hoosier State

Bird: Cardinal

Flower: Peony

The first professional baseball game was played in Fort Wayne, Indiana, on May 4, 1871.

Kentucky (KY)

Capital: Frankfort

Nickname: Bluegrass State

Bird: Cardinal

Flower: Goldenrod

The Kentucky Derby horse race at Churchill Downs began in 1875, and has been held every year since!

Tennessee (TN)

Capital: Nashville

Nickname: Volunteer State

Bird: Mockingbird

Flower: Iris

Wilma Rudolph was called "The Tennessee Tornado." In 1960, she was the first American woman to win three track and field gold medals at one Olympics games.

Michigan (MI)

Capital: Lansing

Nicknames: Wolverine State;
          Great Lakes State

Bird: Robin

Flower: Apple blossom

Detroit, Michigan, is the "Car Capital of the World." Henry Ford started producing cars there in 1913.

Wisconsin (WI)

Capital: Madison

Nickname: Badger State

Bird: Robin

Flower: Wood violet

Wisconsin is called "America's Dairyland." It produces more cheese than any other state.

Minnesota (MN)

Capital: Saint Paul

Nicknames: North Star State;
             Gopher State

Bird: Common loon

Flower: Lady's slipper

Two Minnesota students, Scott and Brennan Olson, used their hockey boots to make the first Rollerblades in 1980.

Iowa (IA)

Capital: Des Moines

Nickname: Hawkeye State

Bird: Eastern goldfinch

Flower: Wild prairie rose

Iowa is called the "Land Where the Tall Corn Grows." It produces more corn than any other state.

Illinois (IL)

Capital: Springfield

Nickname: Prairie State

Bird: Cardinal

Flower: Illinois violet

The world's first skyscraper was built in Chicago, Illinois, in 1885.

Missouri (MO)

Capital: Jefferson City

Nickname: Show Me State

Bird: Bluebird

Flower: White hawthorn blossom

Mark Twain was born in Hannibal, Missouri. He wrote the novels *Tom Sawyer* and *Huckleberry Finn*.

Arkansas (AR)

Capital: Little Rock

Nicknames: Land of Opportunity;
The Natural State

Bird: Mockingbird

Flower: Apple blossom

Arkansas has the only diamond mine in the world open to the public.

Kansas (KS)

Capital: Topeka
Nickname: Sunflower State
Bird: Western meadowlark
Flower: Sunflower

William Purvis and Charles Wilson of Goodland, Kansas, invented the helicopter in 1909.

Oklahoma (OK)

Capital: Oklahoma City
Nickname: Sooner State
Bird: Scissor-tailed flycatcher
Flower: Mistletoe

The National Cowboy Hall of Fame is in Oklahoma City, Oklahoma.

Texas (TX)

Capital: Austin
Nickname: Lone Star State
Bird: Mockingbird
Flower: Bluebonnet

Texas has some of the largest cattle ranches in the world!

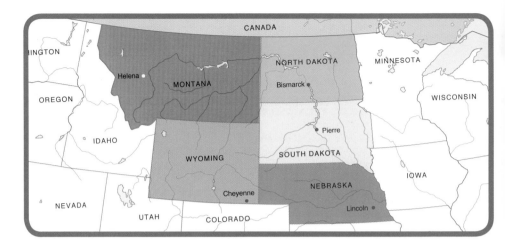

North Dakota (ND)

Capital: Bismarck

Nickname: Flickertail State

Bird: Western meadowlark

Flower: Wild prairie rose

North Dakota grows more sunflowers than any other state.

South Dakota (SD)

Capital: Pierre

Nicknames: Mount Rushmore State; Coyote State

Bird: Ring-necked pheasant

Flower: Pasque (*May Day*) flower

The faces of Presidents George Washington, Thomas Jefferson, Theodore Roosevelt, and Abraham Lincoln are sculpted into Mount Rushmore in South Dakota.

Nebraska (NE)

Capital: Lincoln

Nickname: Cornhusker State

Bird: Western meadowlark

Flower: Goldenrod

The National Liars' Hall of Fame is located in Dannebrog, Nebraska.

Montana (MT)

Capital: Helena

Nickname: Treasure State

Bird: Western meadowlark

Flower: Bitterroot

At Egg Mountain in Montana, a nest of fossilized dinosaur eggs was discovered in 1979.

Wyoming (WY)

Capital: Cheyenne

Nickname: Equality State

Bird: Western meadowlark

Flower: Indian paintbrush

An elementary class on a field trip found a dinosaur skull and bones at Alcova Lake in Wyoming.

Colorado (CO)

Capital: Denver

Nickname: Centennial State

Bird: Lark bunting

Flower: Rocky Mountain columbine

The largest sand dune in North America is found in Great Sand Dunes National Monument in Colorado.

New Mexico (NM)

Capital: Santa Fe

Nickname: Land of Enchantment

Bird: Roadrunner

Flower: Yucca flower

Carlsbad Caverns of New Mexico is home to 300,000 bats.

Arizona (AZ)

Capital: Phoenix
Nickname: Grand Canyon State
Bird: Cactus wren
Flower: Saguaro cactus blossom

Arizona is home to the Grand Canyon, the Painted Desert, Sunset Crater, and the Colorado River.

Utah (UT)

Capital: Salt Lake City
Nickname: Beehive State
Bird: California gull
Flower: Sego lily

In 1848, great flocks of sea gulls flew over from California and ate up crickets that were destroying Utah's crops. It was considered a miracle!

Idaho (ID)

Capital: Boise
Nickname: Gem State
Bird: Mountain bluebird
Flower: Syringa (mock orange)

Idaho is famous for growing potatoes. The Idaho Potato Museum is in the city of Blackfoot.

Nevada (NV)

Capital: Carson City
Nickname: Silver State
Bird: Mountain bluebird
Flower: Sagebrush

Nevada, the Silver State, produces more silver and gold than any other state.

California (CA)

Capital: Sacramento

Nickname: Golden State

Bird: California valley quail

Flower: Golden poppy

The oldest tree in the U.S., a 4800-year-old bristlecone pine called Methuselah, lives in the White Mountains of California.

Oregon (OR)

Capital: Salem

Nickname: Beaver State

Bird: Western meadowlark

Flower: Oregon grape

Crater Lake in Oregon is the deepest lake in the U.S. It formed after the collapse of an ancient volcano.

Washington (WA)

Capital: Olympia

Nickname: Evergreen State

Bird: Willow goldfinch

Flower: Coast rhododendron

Washington grows more apples than any other state.

Alaska (AK)

Capital: Juneau

Nickname: The Last Frontier

Bird: Willow ptarmigan

Flower: Forget-me-not

Alaska is the largest state. It is 656,424 square miles—more than twice the size of Texas.

Hawaii (HI)

Capital: Honolulu

Nickname: Aloha State

Bird: Nene (Hawaiian goose)

Flower: Hibiscus

The native Hawaiian language uses only 12 letters: a, e, i, o, u, h, k, l, m, n, p, w.

. . . .

Six hours after the dawn's early light awakens Eastport, Maine, it shines on the most western parts of our country— Hawaii and the Aleutian Islands of Alaska. What a beautiful, bountiful country the sun warms as it travels across these fifty great states.